Ngari The Hunter

NGARI

The Hunter

RONALD ROSE

HARCOURT, BRACE & WORLD, INC.
NEW YORK

By the same author
INOKE SAILS THE SOUTH SEAS

Most of Australia is dry. In the centre of the continent, there are vast areas of desert and semi-desert country—dry, dusty plains and ridges of bright red sand dotted with prickly spinifex grass, stunted mulga trees, and occasional gum trees. In this country, the most common animals are lizards—fat lizards, thin lizards, spiky lizards, lizards with frilled necks, lizards that drop their tails off when they are touched, ugly lizards, lizards not so ugly, and lizards that burrow deep in the red sand.

Most of the lizards are good to eat, and some of the aboriginal people who live in these desert areas have been called The Lizard Eaters. The aborigines eat other things, of course —snakes, bush turkeys, emus, grass seeds, nuts, berries, and kangaroos when they can get them.

Life was hard for these people when they lived in the tribe. They had to walk long distances between waterholes, and food was often hard to find. Because they were always on the move, these nomads did not build permanent houses. Almost all their lives were spent in the struggle to survive. Even young children could read the animal tracks in the desert sand and know what they meant.

Now, very few aborigines live a tribal life in the lonely Australian outback. There are still some, but most aborigines live on government settlements or missions, where they receive good food and medical care and send their children to school.

One of the most remote of the settlements in the centre of Australia is Papunya—about halfway between the town of Alice Springs and the Western Australian border. One of the children who lives at Papunya is a boy of the Wailbri tribe called Ngari.

Ngari is a hunter. He knows the tracks of all the animals in his tribal country and he knows how to catch many of them. His father made his spear for him. It has a good mulga wood point, made hard and tough in the flames of a fire. As well as animals, Ngari knows how to find all sorts of other food in the arid country that is his home. He calls the animals and the other foods "bush tucker".

Ngari's sister, Nungarai, has fair hair like other aboriginal children in the desert, but it will get darker when she grows up. Nungarai is very good at catching lizards. She follows their tracks in the sand and then digs them out with a digging stick made from the mulga tree.

Tutuma is Ngari's father. He is one of the best hunters of the tribe and often brings back a kangaroo to the camp. Tutuma likes to mix tobacco, or a plant called pituri, with ash and then chew it. He holds some acacia leaves over the fire to make the right sort of ash.

Some aboriginal people call the tribal lands of the Wailbri people "rubbish country" because there are so many stones and not much grass. But to the Wailbri it is good country and the elders of the tribe tell stories about the rocks and the mountains that go right back to the Dream Time, when everything began.

Great flocks of birds, like these pink and grey galahs, screech and chatter in the trees. The aboriginal people do not hunt galahs because they are not very good to eat.

Many people live at Papunya—Wailbris, Pintubis, and
Loritjas, and a few white people, the nurses and school
teachers and the people who run the settlement. The different
aboriginal tribes live in camps around the settlement, but
sometimes the aborigines go on walkabout, back into the old
tribal lands.

The children enjoy playing with the donkeys at Papunya.
Donkeys were brought as pack animals to central Australia by
white people many years ago. Most of them are now wild,
but the Papunya children have caught and tamed some.

Some young men have their own little camp behind a tin windbreak, where they can talk and make spears and boomerangs. Some of the boomerangs have a hook on one end—these are very good for hunting kangaroos. Boomerangs made by aborigines in the centre of Australia do not come back to the thrower; they are used for hunting.

The old men sit together and talk about tribal matters, and they still keep up many of the old customs. In former times there was no string, so the men had to make it from human hair. The old men have a big collection of hair string. With it they will make their headbands and use it for special sacred things that the boys will learn about later when they are initiated into the secrets of the tribe.

In the old days wurlies, or shelters, were made from spinifex grass put on boughs. This old man's wurlie is made from bags and sticks. He is making a coolamon from the trunk of a soft bean tree. Coolamons are shallow dishes used to carry food or water, but mostly the women use them to carry their babies. This man keeps his food in the fork of a tree so that his hunting dogs cannot get it.

At Mt. Larrie, not far from Papunya, there is a big waterhole where the children go swimming. This is the most water any of them has ever seen.

Ngari likes to catch lizards. This one is a mountain devil, which the Wailbri people call a mingari. Although it looks very fierce with its spikes and spines, it is really quite harmless, and Ngari keeps it as a pet.

Some of the big fat lizards move quite slowly, so they are easy to catch. Most desert lizards are good to eat, but kangaroos are the favourite "bush tucker" of these people.

Sometimes Ngari manages to track and catch a goanna, a large lizard, and holds it up by the tail to show his sister. Nungarai watches Ngari carefully because, when they grow up, it will still be her work to catch lizards while, most of the time, Ngari will have more important things to do.

The women of the tribe collect the seeds from different plants, grind them into flour between stones, and cook them into a sort of cake.

Sometimes the children catch animals that are not good to eat. Ngari and his friend Djagamara have found some tiny marsupial mice, which live only in Australia. The mice keep their young in pouches, just like kangaroos.

The best food is kangaroo, and sometimes the boys are allowed to go with the men on their hunting trips. The hunters stalk the kangaroo very carefully and quietly until they get close enough to throw their spears.

Tutuma, Ngari's father, brings back to camp a big red kangaroo he has speared. This means work for Ngari and Nungarai.
They have to dig a pit to cook the kangaroo and gather wood
for the fire. When the fire is lit, Ngari makes sure that it does
not go out.

Ngari sees something small moving in the bushes nearby. He moves stealthily towards it, taking care to make no sound, and sees a young kangaroo, a joey. He takes the joey by surprise and catches it firmly by the tail. The joey was probably thrown from her pouch by the mother kangaroo so that she could escape more easily from the hunters.

Ngari is delighted. Now he has two pets—a lizard and a young kangaroo.

On special occasions the men of the tribe have a corroboree. Often it is after a successful kangaroo hunt, or when some of the traditional ceremonies of the tribe are carried out. The men decorate themselves with paints of red, yellow, and white made from ground-up rocks or clay mixed with kangaroo fat.

The painted designs have special meanings and show which totem, or group of the tribe, each man belongs to. When they sing their corroboree songs, the men beat time with boomerangs and digging sticks.

The boys also paint themselves. They use a black powder that they find inside a small plant with a silvery coat which is like a mushroom. There is very little in the desert for which the aborigines do not find a use.

One morning, when Ngari and Nungarai are sitting in their wurlie talking about the big kangaroo hunt, some of their friends ask them to come and play games. Ngari decides to go away on his own. It is hot, so he takes off his shirt and goes into the sand hills to look for animal tracks.

On and on he walks, into strange places he has heard about but never seen before, the "dreaming places", which are the sources of aboriginal legends, the stories that started in the Dream Time and are passed down from generation to generation. He sees the dreaming place of the willy wagtail, the little black bird with the long, swishy tail. The aboriginal legend says that, back in the Dream Time, the ancestor willy wagtail swept his tail and made the great marks in the rocks.

It is rough country, but Ngari's homeland, a country full of mystery and stories. To the aborigines, these rocks tell the story of a man, a woman, and the moon.

Once Ngari sees a carpet python sliding along a branch towards an owl-like bird called a mopoke. The mopoke is sitting very still and trying to look like a dead branch but Ngari feels sure the snake will not be fooled by this, so he chases it away.

Sometimes a group of ghost gums, their white ghostly limbs
gleaming, stand in Ngari's path.

In the red sand, where the clumps of spinifex grow, Ngari finds an ant-hill, looking like some strange castle. The aborigines call spinifex "porcupine grass" because of its spikes. The men burn it and get a black sticky substance from the ashes; they use this to stick the stone points onto their spears or to make handles for their throwing sticks.

Back at the camp the old men grow worried about Ngari's long absence. They sit solemnly in a circle and listen to Tutuma. He decides to organise a search.

Two of Ngari's special friends set out on one of the donkeys to look for him. After they have gone a little way, they leave the donkey behind and circle around looking for marks made by Ngari—tracks, bushes pushed aside, crushed insects, or stones out of place.

They see many messages in the sand: trails made by ants; red mounds built by the desert centipedes; and the tracks of bush turkeys.

Meanwhile, to keep away the chill of the evening, Ngari makes himself a fire by rubbing two dry sticks together. He feels happier with a fire to keep him company, too!

Ngari's two friends are still searching for signs and at last, in the sandy country, they find the tracks they are looking for.

By this time Ngari's fire is getting low and he is beginning to feel rather small and lonely. Perhaps he should not have strayed so far from Papunya.

Suddenly Ngari's friends run up to him with whoops of joy. They are all glad to see each other and decide to settle down for the night by the remains of the fire. They will find their way back to the donkey, and the settlement, in the morning.

Ngari is surprised to hear from his friends of the trouble he has caused. He tells them that he has not been lost. If he had been lost, he would have lit a big spinifex fire which makes black smoke, and left plenty of marks to help people find him. Next morning the boys set off towards home.

There is much excitement in the camp when the boys return. Everyone runs out to welcome them.

And all day, as they play together, Ngari keeps telling his sister, Nungarai, that he had not really been lost at all. He had just been for a little walkabout in the bush.